NTSB/RAR-08/02
PB2008-916302
Notation 7853A
Adopted May 13, 2008

I0428078

Railroad Accident Report

Derailment of Norfolk Southern Railway Company Train 68QB119
with Release of Hazardous Materials and Fire
New Brighton, Pennsylvania
October 20, 2006

**National
Transportation
Safety Board**

490 L'Enfant Plaza, S.W.
Washington, D.C. 20594

National Transportation Safety Board. 2008. *Derailment of Norfolk Southern Railway Company Train 68QB119 with Release of Hazardous Materials and Fire, New Brighton, Pennsylvania, October 20, 2006.* Railroad Accident Report NTSB/RAR-08/02. Washington, DC.

Abstract: About 10:41 p.m. eastern daylight time on Friday, October 20, 2006, Norfolk Southern Railway Company train 68QB119, en route from the Chicago, Illinois, area to Sewaren, New Jersey, derailed while crossing the Beaver River railroad bridge in New Brighton, Pennsylvania. The train consisted of a three-unit locomotive pulling 3 empty freight cars followed by 83 tank cars loaded with denatured ethanol, a flammable liquid. Twenty-three of the tank cars derailed near the east end of the bridge, with several of the cars falling into the Beaver River. Of the 23 derailed tank cars, about 20 released ethanol, which subsequently ignited and burned for about 48 hours. Some of the unburned ethanol liquid was released into the river and the surrounding soil. Homes and businesses within a seven-block area of New Brighton and in an area adjacent to the accident were evacuated for 2 days. No injuries or fatalities resulted from the accident. The Norfolk Southern Railway Company estimated total damages to be $5.8 million.

The safety issues identified in this accident are ultrasonic rail inspection and rail defect management, oversight of the internal rail inspection process and requirements for internal rail inspection, and the placement of hazardous materials cars in trains for crew protection.

As a result of its investigation of this accident, the National Transportation Safety Board makes recommendations to the Federal Railroad Administration, the Pipeline and Hazardous Materials Safety Administration, and the Norfolk Southern Railway Company

Contents

ACRONYMS AND ABBREVIATIONS

AAR	Association of American Railroads
CFR	*Code of Federal Regulations*
CSX	CSX Corporation
DOT	U.S. Department of Transportation
F	Fahrenheit
FRA	Federal Railroad Administration
mgt	million gross tons
MW&S	Maintenance of Way and Structures
NS	Norfolk Southern Railway Company
PHMSA	Pipeline and Hazardous Materials Safety Administration
psi	pounds per square inch
RSAC	Rail Safety Advisory Committee
Sperry	Sperry Rail Service
Transcaer	Transportation Community Awareness and Emergency Response
TTCI	Transportation Technology Center, Inc.
UP	Union Pacific Railroad

EXECUTIVE SUMMARY

About 10:41 p.m. eastern daylight time on Friday, October 20, 2006, Norfolk Southern Railway Company train 68QB119, en route from the Chicago, Illinois, area to Sewaren, New Jersey, derailed while crossing the Beaver River railroad bridge in New Brighton, Pennsylvania. The train consisted of a three-unit locomotive pulling 3 empty freight cars followed by 83 tank cars loaded with denatured ethanol, a flammable liquid. Twenty-three of the tank cars derailed near the east end of the bridge, with several of the cars falling into the Beaver River. Of the 23 derailed tank cars, about 20 released ethanol, which subsequently ignited and burned for about 48 hours. Some of the unburned ethanol liquid was released into the river and the surrounding soil. Homes and businesses within a seven-block area of New Brighton and in an area adjacent to the accident were evacuated for 2 days. No injuries or fatalities resulted from the accident. The Norfolk Southern Railway Company estimated total damages to be $5.8 million.

The National Transportation Safety Board determines that the probable cause of the derailment of Norfolk Southern Railway Company train 68QB119 was the Norfolk Southern Railway Company's inadequate rail inspection and maintenance program that resulted in a rail fracture from an undetected internal defect. Contributing to the accident were the Federal Railroad Administration's inadequate oversight of the internal rail inspection process and its insufficient requirements for internal rail inspection.

As a result of its investigation of this accident, the Safety Board identified the following safety issues:

- Ultrasonic rail inspection and rail defect management,
- Oversight of the internal rail inspection process and requirements for internal rail inspection, and
- The placement of hazardous materials cars in trains for crew protection.

As a result of its investigation of this accident, the National Transportation Safety Board makes recommendations to the Federal Railroad Administration, the Pipeline and Hazardous Materials Safety Administration, and the Norfolk Southern Railway Company.

FACTUAL INFORMATION

Accident Synopsis

About 10:41 p.m. eastern daylight time on Friday, October 20, 2006, eastbound[1] Norfolk Southern Railway Company (NS) train 68QB119, en route from the Chicago, Illinois, area to Sewaren, New Jersey, derailed while crossing the Beaver River railroad bridge on main track 1 near a milepost designated PC 29.26[2] in New Brighton, Pennsylvania. The train consisted of a three-unit locomotive pulling 3 empty freight cars followed by 83 tank cars loaded with denatured ethanol, a flammable liquid. Twenty-three of the tank cars, the 23rd through 45th, derailed near the east end of the bridge, with several of the cars falling into the Beaver River. (See figure 1.) Of the 23 derailed tank cars, about 20 released ethanol, which subsequently ignited and burned for about 48 hours. Some of the unburned ethanol liquid was released into the river and the surrounding soil. Homes and businesses within a seven-block area of New Brighton and in an area adjacent to the accident were evacuated for 2 days. No injuries or fatalities resulted from the accident. The NS estimated total damages to be $5.8 million.

The Accident

The train originated on October 18, 2006, on the Union Pacific Railroad (UP) in Eagle Grove, Iowa, as UP train UEEBNF-16. The UP train was interchanged to the NS at the UP's Proviso Yard near Chicago, Illinois, and became NS train 68QB119 destined for Sewaren, New Jersey. The train was considered a "relay" (run-through) train because it would remain intact with the equipment as interchanged from the UP in Chicago.

After an initial terminal air brake test and equipment inspection, the accident train departed Chicago at 11:30 p.m. on October 19, 2006. At Elkhart, Indiana, the first NS crew change point, an NS locomotive unit equipped with cab signals was added to the head of the train.[3] At that point, the train had 3 locomotive units, 3 empty freight cars, and 83 DOT-111A general service tank cars containing ethanol. It had a trailing tonnage of 10,745 tons and a length of 5,327 feet. The train consist remained unchanged.

---

[1] In this report all train movements and track references will refer to timetable direction.

[2] The track milepost numbering increases in the westward direction.

[3] Cab signal units display the governing signal indication in the cab of the locomotive. The territory where the accident occurred utilized cab signals; it was not equipped with wayside signals except at control points.

Figure 1. View of derailment. NS train 68QB119 was traveling from left to right.

The two-person (engineer and conductor) train crew went on duty in Toledo, Ohio, at 2:30 p.m. on October 20. They boarded the train at 4:20 p.m. and departed Toledo at 4:30 p.m.

The crew described their trip as normal up to and including the time the head end of the train, which was being operated under a *clear*[4] signal indication, traversed the NS bridge spanning the Beaver River in New Brighton, Pennsylvania. The engineer stated that about 200 yards after his locomotive came off the east end of the bridge, his cab signal indication went from *clear* to *approach.*[5] The engineer had been using braking to control the train's speed. He said that his train had traveled another 200 to 300 yards when the train's brakes activated with an emergency application. According to the locomotive event recorder, this occurred about 10:41:23 p.m. while the train was traveling 37 mph. At 10:41:57 p.m., based on the event recorder speed data, the train came to a complete stop. The locomotive came to rest about a half mile past the east end of the Beaver River bridge. The crew said they did not see or feel any irregularities before the emergency brake application.

The crewmembers said that they were not immediately aware that a derailment had occurred, but that they saw a bright flash toward the rear of their train. Using the locomotive radio, the engineer contacted the NS Cleveland Line

---

[4] A *clear* indication signals the engineer to proceed not exceeding normal speed (maximum authorized speed).

[5] An *approach* indication signals the engineer to proceed prepared to stop at the next signal.

dispatcher and said, "We got a fire here ... I think we had an explosion." The dispatcher told the crew to evacuate the area, after which the two crewmembers walked eastward until they were about 1/2 mile away from the head of the train. At 10:45 p.m., the engineer called 911 from his cell phone and reported that he had a train with 80 cars of ethanol and that there had been an explosion. He reported that the train was on the bridge just west of New Brighton. The conductor used his cell phone to call the NS supervisor of train operations.

After providing hand-written statements to NS officials, the crewmembers were transported to Heritage Valley Health Systems Medical Center in Beaver, Pennsylvania, where they were tested for drugs and alcohol in accordance with Federal Railroad Administration (FRA) postaccident requirements. The train crew was relieved at 2:29 a.m. on October 21, 2006, and went off duty at 3:52 a.m.

Emergency Response

The Beaver County Emergency Services Center received the first 911 notification of the accident at 10:42 p.m. from an unidentified cell phone caller. The caller reported that a train had derailed off the bridge into the river and that there was a massive fire. The New Brighton Borough fire chief was at a nearby residence; he stated that he heard two large "swooshes" and responded to the area immediately.

At 10:45, the 911 operator received the call from the train engineer reporting the explosion. At 10:47 p.m., the NS Cleveland Line dispatcher called the New Brighton area 911 to report a train on fire just east of Beaver Falls; the 911 operator advised that emergency response personnel were already responding to the accident (a total of 158 calls were received within a short time of the accident). At 10:52 p.m., the NS police communications center confirmed the notification with the 911 operator and, at 11:05 p.m., faxed a copy of the train consist to the Emergency Services Center. The NS assistant division superintendent was notified, and he responded to the incident command post with the train consist. He arrived on scene about 11:30 p.m.

Emergency responders established a command post, staging area, rehab area,[6] and accountability group[7] in the accident vicinity. New Brighton fire and police department personnel went door-to-door and evacuated persons in New Brighton. In Beaver Falls, emergency responders evacuated residents of Bridge Street. The initial evacuation zone in New Brighton was from the river to 5th Street and 5th Avenue. This zone was subsequently expanded from the river to 8th Street and 7th Avenue. The evacuation was estimated to have affected about 150 people. Evacuees were directed to the First Methodist Church, the New Brighton Middle School cafeteria, or the Patterson Township Fire Department. (See figure 2.)

---

[6] The *rehab area* is a location where responders can get rest, food, and drink.

[7] The *accountability group* was responsible for tracking personnel coming into and out of the accident area.

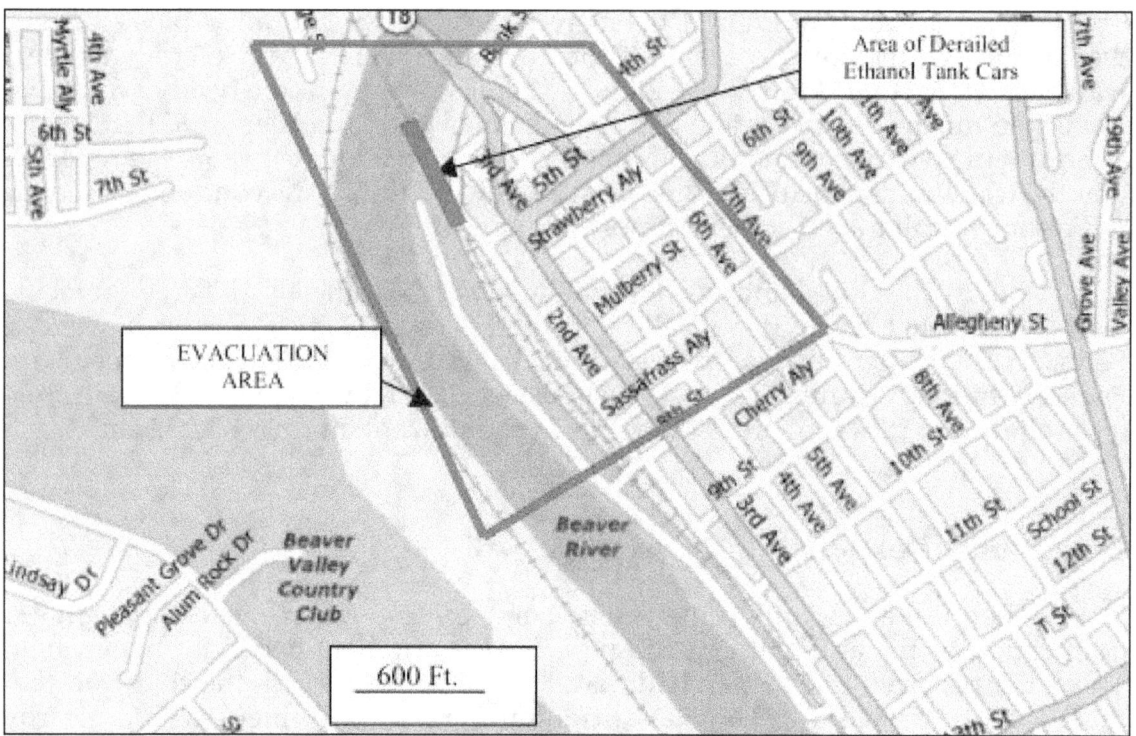

Figure 2. Limits of New Brighton evacuation area.

The incident commander suspended railroad traffic on the CSX Corporation (CSX) tracks north and across the river from the derailment site. The tracks were returned to operation at 10:00 a.m. on Saturday, October 21.

Firefighters staged in a parking lot near the north (railroad west) end of the bridge. From this position, they did not have a good view of the cars that fell off the bridge. Firefighters began defensive operations by setting up water supply lines and applying an unmanned fog spray to the house nearest to the bridge because of the heat generated by the fire. Water streams were not immediately sprayed onto the railcars because of concerns about the cars' structural integrity.

Overnight, fire command decided to continue defensive operations, monitor conditions, and allow the fires to burn overnight. On Saturday morning, October 21, two teams consisting of firefighters and railroad hazardous materials responders (including NS contractors and NS environmental protection and hazardous materials personnel) entered the accident area to assess the condition of the site and the tank cars.

Wreck clearing and off-loading of ethanol from some tank cars began Saturday evening. By Sunday morning, October 22, wrecking crews had removed eight cars from the riverbank and eight cars from the track area. All fires were extinguished by 11:15 p.m. on Sunday. On Monday morning shortly after 9:00 a.m., emergency response activities were concluded, and residents were allowed to return to their homes. The last derailed car had been removed by 12:50 p.m.

Of the 660,952 gallons of ethanol that had been loaded into the 23 derailed tank cars, about 175,674 gallons were recovered. About 485,278 gallons of product were estimated to have been released. A January 2007 report prepared by the environmental consulting firm ENSR Corporation and submitted to the Pennsylvania Department of Environmental Protection on behalf of the NS stated that the fire consumed most of the ethanol released, and that the exact volume of ethanol released to the soil or into the Beaver River could not be determined. The report also stated that any release into the Beaver River did not result in observable negative effects such as fish kills or sheen on the river, and no downstream water treatment facilities were affected. The Department of Environmental Protection approved the report on January 31, 2007.

Postaccident Site Inspection

Safety Board investigators found no track anomalies or evidence of dragging equipment west of the location between a destroyed track section near milepost PC 29.26 and milepost PC 30.5 on main track 1. Based on the footprint[8] of the derailment, investigators determined the point of derailment to be the north rail at milepost PC 29.26. At this location, investigators found pieces of broken rail under the last derailed car, some of which exhibited markings consistent with rail-end batter.[9] A total of seven segments of broken rail were recovered east of milepost PC 29.26 and sent to the Safety Board's Materials Laboratory for further examination. (The results of these examinations are detailed in the "Tests and Research" section of this report.) Five rail defects described as "detail fracture from shelling"[10] (also called a *shell crack*) were visibly evident on the fracture faces of the rail head segments. (See figure 3.)

---

[8] The *footprint* included visible evidence such as marks on the ties, marks on the track components and rails, and car and truck component positions and conditions.

[9] *Batter* is the deformation of the surface of the rail head, usually close to the end of the rail. *Receiving rail-end batter* is a deformation of the rail head caused when an oncoming wheel strikes the rail end. *Trailing rail-end batter* deformation occurs when the wheel rolls over and off the rail head end.

[10] The Sperry Rail Service *Rail Defect Manual* defines a *detail fracture from shelling* as a progressive fracture (fatigue crack) starting from a longitudinal separation close to the running surface of the rail head, then turning downward to form a transverse separation substantially at right angles to the running surface. *Shelling* is surface cracking by metal fatigue near the gage corner caused by repetitive shearing stresses. It is a progressive separation that may crack out at any level on the gage side of the rail but generally at the gage corner.

Figure 3. Recovered rail showing detail fracture from shelling in head area.

Injuries

No injuries occurred as a result of the accident.

Damages

Tank Car Damages

Safety Board investigators inspected the derailed ethanol tank cars after they had been moved to a work site adjacent to the tracks in New Brighton's Big Rock Park. Of the 23 tank cars that derailed, 12 lost their full loads of about 28,700 gallons of ethanol. Eight other tank cars lost partial loads ranging from 20 gallons to 27,613 gallons.

Twelve tank cars received extensive shell damage, including eight tank cars that fell from the bridge following the derailment and lost their entire contents. Heat from the fire caused one additional tank car to overpressurize and rupture. Eight additional cars lost product from their fittings, valves, and connectors during the fire following the derailment.

Track and Structure Damages

The east bridge spans of both tracks sustained minor damage to the steel supporting structures and substantial damage to the concrete supporting decks. About 990 feet of tracks 1 and 2 were destroyed.

Monetary Damages

The NS estimated monetary damages from the accident as $1,985,000 for the damaged tank cars; $882,919 for track, structures, and signals; and $354,432 for nonhazardous materials derailment cleanup. The estimated cost of lost product/ lading, emergency response/remediation, environmental site remediation, and incidental costs was $2,546,304. These estimated damages totaled $5,768,655.

Personnel Information

Accident Train Engineer

The accident train engineer began service as a brakeman with Conrail on May 17, 1999, and transferred to the NS on June 1, 1999. He became an engineer on October 20, 2002, and had 4 years' experience as an engineer at the time of the accident. On his last rules examination, in May 2003, he was commended for a perfect score. He passed his last engineer's certification on March 7, 2006. He was assigned to the extra list[11] working from Conway yard.

Accident Train Conductor

The accident train conductor had 4 years of service. He started with the NS on October 3, 2002, and was promoted to conductor on April 10, 2003. He was assigned to work between Conway yard and Toledo, Ohio. He estimated that he had made between 200 and 300 round trips between Conway yard and Toledo without incident.

NS Track Supervisor

The NS track supervisor at Conway, Pennsylvania,[12] was the NS front line manager responsible for track maintenance and inspection on the portion of the territory where the accident occurred. The NS track supervisor at Conway began working with the Penn Central Railroad in 1972 as a track laborer and stayed in

---

[11] The *extra list*, or *extra board*, is a pool of employees assigned to jobs as needed either to substitute for a regular employee who is unavailable for duty or to serve as a crewmember on an unscheduled assignment.

[12] Conway yard is about 6 miles south of New Brighton and is a major NS train yard terminal and maintenance facility.

that job for about 2 years. He then worked as a track foreman and an assistant supervisor. He was promoted to track supervisor at Wellsville, Ohio, in 1976 and at Conway in 1984. Beginning in 1992, he worked in assets management and projects for about 5 years. When the NS purchased Penn Central Railroad assets from Conrail in the late 1990s, he was reassigned as an assistant track supervisor and in November 2004 was promoted to track supervisor at Conway.

NS Assistant Track Supervisor

The NS assistant track supervisor at Conway had inspected the track in the accident area on the day of the accident. The assistant track supervisor had 14 years of railroad experience, having started working for Conrail on April 26, 1992. He worked various positions in the track department, beginning with track laborer, then assistant foreman and foreman. After he completed an NS supervisory training program in 2004, he was promoted to assistant track supervisor in Danville, Virginia. In April 2006, he was promoted to assistant track supervisor at Conway. The position required him to perform FRA-required track and switch inspections.

Sperry Ultrasonic Rail Inspection Chief Operator

The Sperry Rail Service (Sperry) chief operator, who had conducted the last ultrasonic rail inspection before the accident,[13] started work with the company on June 22, 2002. After 28 weeks of on-the-job training, he completed a corporate track safety certification course during which he continued his training on actual railroad tracks. He then worked for 2 years with a qualified operator to gain additional experience. He passed the operator's examination in 2003 and passed the chief operator's examination in 2004. In September 2004, after completing 40 hours of training at Sperry's offices in Danbury, Connecticut, he obtained his ultrasonic level one certification.[14] He became a chief operator in June 2005.

Work/Rest History

Safety Board investigators developed a 96-hour work/rest history for both the engineer and the conductor. The investigation determined that at the time of the accident, the engineer had been on duty for 8 hours 11 minutes and had been continuously awake for a little more than 14 hours. The conductor was determined to have been on duty for about 8 hours 11 minutes when the accident occurred and had been continuously awake for about 11 hours 41 minutes.

---

[13] Sperry had contracted with the NS to conduct an internal inspection of the accident track in 2006.

[14] The American Railway Engineering and Maintenance of Way Association Committee 4, Rail, recommends that operators achieve this certification to learn basic knowledge of ultrasonic/nondestructive testing.

Toxicological Information

In accordance with 49 *Code of Federal Regulations* (CFR) Part 219, Subpart C, "FRA Post-Accident Toxicological Testing," toxicological specimens were obtained from the engineer and the conductor of train 68QB119. The tests screened for substances including cannabinoids, cocaine, opiates, amphetamines, methamphetamines, phencyclidine, barbiturates, benzodiazepines, and ethyl alcohol. For both the engineer and the conductor, the results were negative for the presence of any of the tested drugs or for alcohol.

Meteorological Information

The closest weather stations to the accident site were Pittsburgh International Airport – about 23 miles south of New Brighton with weather data from 10:51 p.m. – and the Beaver County Airport – about 5 miles northwest of New Brighton with weather data from 8:49 p.m. The stations recorded 7 miles visibility, winds calm to 6 knots from the west-southwest, mostly cloudy skies, and a temperature of about 42° Fahrenheit (F).

Site Description

The accident occurred in New Brighton, Pennsylvania, on the NS bridge over the Beaver River about 26 miles northwest of Pittsburgh, Pennsylvania. The 2004 United States Census showed a population of 17,231 for New Brighton and the area surrounding the derailment.

Track

The derailment occurred on the NS Pittsburgh Division's Fort Wayne Line on track 1 about milepost PC 29.26. This portion of the Fort Wayne Line had double main-line tracks. The NS designated this segment as a "key route."[15] It was maintained to Class 4 track standards with a maximum authorized timetable speed of 50 mph for freight trains and 79 mph for passenger trains.

The NS tracks are located on a fill between the New Brighton business district and a community park adjacent to the Beaver River. The CSX Pittsburgh Subdivision tracks are located on the west side of the Beaver River and cross under the NS tracks north of New Brighton. The NS Youngstown Line is located north of

---

[15] The Association of American Railroads defines a *key route* as "any track with a combination of 10,000 car loads or intermodal portable tank loads of hazardous materials, or a combination of 4,000 car loadings of [poisonous inhalation hazard] or [toxic inhalation hazard] (Hazard zone A, B, C, or D), anhydrous ammonia, flammable gas, Class 1.1 or 1.2 explosives, environmentally sensitive chemicals, [spent nuclear fuel], and [high-level radioactive waste] over a period of 1 year."

New Brighton on the east side of the Beaver River, and it connects to the NS main tracks east of New Brighton. East of the bridge was a tunnel, PC-29.2, over the NS Youngstown Line, which was not damaged or involved in the accident, but the derailed cars also spanned the tunnel.

NS records for the full length of track 1 showed that the line carried 63.5 million gross tons (mgt) per year. About 70 NS freight trains and 2 scheduled Amtrak passenger trains operated daily over the accident portion of the Fort Wayne Line. The NS estimated that about 29 mgt had moved across the accident area in the 6 1/2 months preceding the accident.

The track structure conformed to NS standards for continuous welded rail on timber ties. It was anchored every other tie, fastened to steel tie plates with two rail-holding spikes and one tie-holding spike per tie plate, and it had about 23 inches of ballast from the bottom of the tie to the top of the concrete bridge deck. The rail was 140-pound continuous welded rail rolled in 1976 and installed in 1977.

Investigators took track geometry measurements of track 1 at 14 stations. Measurements were taken every 15.5 feet starting at the identified point of derailment, milepost PC 29.26, and continued west, and no exceptions were noted.

Signals

Train movements through the area of the derailment were governed by signal indications of a traffic control system controlled by a computer-aided train dispatching facility under the direction of the NS Cleveland Line train dispatcher at Greentree, Pennsylvania. The system primarily used cab signals (signal indications displayed in the cab of a train's lead locomotive unit); no wayside signals were present except at control points.

Bridge

The NS Beaver River bridge is a 10-span steel and concrete-ballasted deck bridge that spans both the river and the CSX railroad tracks. The top of the rail is about 35 feet above the river. The 1,314-foot-long bridge was built for the Pennsylvania Railroad in 1926 by the Mount Vernon Bridge Company. Two parallel bridge structures support a double main track with the track on the south side of the bridge designated track 1 and the track on the north side designated track 2. The train derailed at the eastern end of the bridge where the two main tracks that cross the bridge begin curving away from each other on separate bridge spans. (See figure 4.)

Figure 4. View of derailment showing track layout and curved track.

Postaccident Inspections

Signal Inspection

Investigators examined signal system data, cab signal equipment from the lead locomotives, and dispatching logs. No exceptions were noted, and postaccident testing of the signal system indicated that the system was working as designed and that the *clear* and *approach* signals received by the locomotive before the derailment were the correct signals for the conditions.

Signal systems utilize the rails as conduits for electrical circuits. Therefore, a signal system may detect a broken rail if the rail ends are separated and the discontinuity does not occur where a track component such as a tie plate could bridge the discontinuity. In this case, the signal system did not detect a discontinuity in the rail before the accident.

Mechanical Inspection

The accident train passed a wheel impact load detector near Vine Creek, Indiana, about 347 miles west of New Brighton. The detector measures the impact of each wheel on the rail and compares impacts between wheels for shifted loads. No exceptions were noted, and all wheel impact forces were determined to be within NS tolerances.

The train passed a hotbox[16] and dragging equipment detector at 10:04 p.m., about 37 minutes and 21 miles before the accident. No exceptions were noted. At 10:39 p.m., about 2 minutes and 1.3 miles before the derailment, the train passed another hotbox and dragging equipment detector, again with no exceptions noted.

The derailment separated the train into three sections. The first section comprised the 3 locomotive units and the first 22 nonderailed cars; the second was made up of the 23 derailed cars; the third section was the rear 41 nonderailed cars. After the accident, the NS moved the first section about 6 miles to Conway yard and moved the rear section westward to Beaver Falls.

Safety Board investigators inspected the 3 locomotives and the first 22 nonderailed cars at the NS Conway yard. The units were used to supply air for a service air brake application measurement. A 27-psi (pounds per square inch) reduction was made on the 90-pound train line brake pipe, and each car's piston travel was measured. All measurements met FRA requirements. The Safety Board investigators then inspected the 41 nonderailed cars at Beaver Falls in the same manner and did not find any significant defects.

Track and Rail Inspection

Two types of inspections will be discussed in this section: track inspections and internal rail inspections. The track inspections are visual inspections that look at the track structure (including ballast, crossties, track assembly fittings, and the physical conditions of rails), the roadbed and areas immediately adjacent to the roadbed, and the track geometry to determine whether these meet Federal and company requirements. Track inspections are to be made on foot or by riding over the track in a vehicle at a speed that allows the person making the inspection to visually inspect the track structure. Mechanical, electrical, and other track inspection devices may be used to supplement visual inspections.

Railroads inspect rail for internal defects using ultrasonic and induction inspection devices either on a specialized inspection vehicle or manually using handheld equipment. In ultrasonic inspection, a transducer emits ultrasonic sound waves that penetrate the rail from various angles. Rail defects, such as cracks in the steel, and rail features[17] will normally reflect the sound waves back to the transducers, and the reflected signals are displayed on a monitor. The equipment operator assesses these reflected signals to identify the cause of the reflection, which could be a crack or other rail defect or a rail feature. In induction inspection, coils moving along the rail at a fixed distance above the rail head detect and measure any distortion within the magnetic field, and this distortion is then assessed by the equipment operator.

---

[16] A *hotbox* is an overheated wheel axle bearing on a railcar.

[17] *Rail features* include bolt holes, welds, and joint bars.

Railroads and rail inspection contractors typically use similar ultrasonic inspection equipment, although differences exist in data processing speed, the presentation of information, and vehicle configuration and setup. During these inspections, data from transducers and induction coils are assessed by the equipment operator. If the operator considers an indication suspect, the inspection vehicle is stopped and backed up to the location of the indication. The operator may then exit the vehicle and inspect the rail by hand using an inspection set mounted on the rear of the car. If a defect is confirmed, it is marked, and a rail work crew following the inspection car can repair or remove the defective rail or ensure that the area is protected.[18] Detail fractures from shelling are difficult to detect using these inspection methods because shelling can impede both the transfer of ultrasonic signals into the specimen and the reflection of the signals back to the detector. Other rail conditions, such as head checks[19] and spalling,[20] and the presence of excess rail lubricants also impede the detection of rail defects.

Sperry representatives said that hand inspection may be more likely to detect a detail fracture from shelling. When performing a hand inspection with a 70° transducer, the operator may be able to orient the transducer sufficiently to get signal penetration underneath some of the surface condition. The vehicle performing the inspection does not have the capability to orient the transducer in this way.

In 1999, the Transportation Technology Center, Inc., (TTCI) conducted a controlled study of rail flaw detection technology.[21] Six inspection vehicles representing a variety of manufacturers were tested on rail with various types and sizes of known defects. The study found that the overall probability of detecting a flaw increased with increasing flaw size. (See table 1.)

Table 1. Probability of defect detection.[a]

Defect Size (as % of Rail Head)	Probability of Detecting Defect
5	58%
10	68%
25	85%
> 60	> 95%

[a] Values from Jeffrey and Peterson, 1999, graph 8.

---

[18] Depending on the type of rail defect identified, protection can include rail replacement, application of joint bars, operating speed restriction, or re-inspection of the rail at regular intervals.

[19] *Head checks* are small hairline cracks in the gage (inside) corner of the rail head.

[20] *Spalling* is the breaking out of metal pieces from the gage corner of the rail head.

[21] B.D. Jeffrey and M.L. Peterson, *Assessment of Rail Flaw Inspection Data*, Colorado State University, disseminated under sponsorship of the U.S. Department of Transportation, University Transportation Centers Program, August 1999.

NS Track Inspection and Maintenance History

Safety Board investigators reviewed the NS track inspection records for the track segment between mileposts PC 20.4 and PC 34.5 for the period from June 1, 2006, to October 20, 2006. Records showed that the inspection frequency complied with the FRA Track Safety Standards.[22]

The accident track had been visually inspected by an NS track inspector in a hy-rail inspection vehicle[23] earlier on the day of the accident. No track defects were noted on the inspection record. The track had been inspected with a track geometry vehicle[24] on October 2, 2006, with no track geometry defects noted for track 1 on the bridge.

The most recent track work in the accident area included rail head grinding (using rotating grinding wheels to remove metal from the rail head) on April 9, 2006, and track surfacing, adjusting alignment, and leveling on October 10, 2006.

Rail grinding is a technique used to control rail profile and manage wheel/rail contact stresses. A rail car wheel rolls on a small contact area of the rail head, and this type of contact loading can lead to rail surface conditions such as head checks, spalling, flaking,[25] and shelling. While these surface conditions are not considered defects, they can serve as features that initiate internal defects, such as transverse defects,[26] and can impede the detection of internal defects during internal rail inspections. Detail fractures from shelling are particularly susceptible to detection problems during ultrasonic inspections, because the shelling from which this type of detail fracture initiates can impede the penetration and return of sound waves through the rail head. Rail grinding is intended to control these rail surface conditions so they will not lead to internal rail defects and rail failures.

The NS monitored the rail profiles at several sites of a test route[27] (the derailment area was not part of the test route). The NS found that rails that were subjected to corrective rail grinding experienced a dramatic increase in wear immediately after each rail-grinding event but returned to a steady wear rate after a short time. The NS determined that too much metal was being removed from the

---

[22] The FRA "Track Safety Standards" (49 CFR 213.233) require that Class 4 track be inspected at least twice weekly with a specified interval between inspections.

[23] A *hy-rail* vehicle, or hy-rail, is a truck that has flanged wheels attached to the front and rear so it can travel over railroad tracks and easily get on or off the track at a road crossing.

[24] Track geometry vehicles are capable of a continuous loaded measurement of gage, track cross level, track alignment, track warp, and ride quality.

[25] *Flaking* is a progressive separation of small, thin pieces of the running surface, often near the gage corner.

[26] *Transverse defects* are progressive cracks oriented perpendicular to the length of the rail.

[27] Stephen S. Woody, "Applying Quality Concepts to the Wheel/Rail Interface," *Interface: The Journal of Wheel/Rail Interaction,* October 2007, http://www.interfacejournal.com/features/10-07/quality/1.html, accessed on October 2, 2007.

rail head during the grinding operations. The excessive grinding was removing the work-hardened layer of the rail, resulting in as-ground rail profiles that were not stable.

In 2006, the NS began work to stabilize the rail profiles on its system by prioritizing routes and determining a grinding frequency. It also began using a rail profile measuring system to perform pregrind inspections and to select a grinding pattern that would produce the best finished profile without removing the work-hardened layer. The track supervisor responsible for track maintenance in the derailment area said he did not notice an increase in rail defects after the rail in that area was ground.

NS Internal Rail Inspection History

The NS contracted with Sperry to inspect track 1 for internal rail defects four times per year, or an interval of about 16 mgt between inspections. This inspection frequency was determined based on a point system model developed for the NS that takes into account track speed, annual tonnage, whether or not hazardous materials are transported over the route, whether the territory is signaled or nonsignaled, rail weight and age, curvature, and rail defect/failure history.

An April 27, 2005, letter from the NS had informed Sperry of the implementation of new inspection procedures for the detection of vertically oriented rail head defects. The NS letter stated that "vertically oriented longitudinal rail head defects can be classified into two types: vertical split heads[28] and shear breaks[29]," which, the letter stated, are similar in appearance.

The new NS procedure for detecting vertical defects included the following point:

> Any rail tested that does not encompass an area where a switch component or track structure is present (point, frog, etc.), and produces a zero degree ultrasonic loss of bottom equipment response [indicating less than full vertical signal penetration] exceeding *five feet in length or greater* [Emphasis added], alone or in conjunction with another test channel, is to be repeated (rerun) by the detector car operator. All efforts are to be made to clear any equipment responses of this nature that are caused by alignment or foreign matter (grease, snow debris, etc.).

---

[28] A *vertical split head* is a progressive longitudinal fracture in the head of the rail where separation along an internal seam, segregation, or inclusion propagates vertically through the rail head.

[29] A *shear break* is a longitudinal separation of the rail head typical to a rail with a sufficient amount of rail head material loss due to mechanical forces and is not typically associated with inherent conditions resulting from the manufacturing process.

Sperry had conducted three ultrasonic/induction inspections for internal rail defects on the accident track in 2006 before the derailment, on January 20, April 18, and August 1. A fourth inspection was scheduled for November. The January 20 inspection revealed no internal rail defects. The April 18 inspection found three rail defects on track 1, two of them on the bridge: one at milepost PC 29.279, and one at milepost PC 29.2565. The August 1 inspection, the last internal rail inspection before the accident, found one rail defect on track 1, at milepost PC 29.271 on the bridge. All of these defects were repaired the same day they were found.

According to interviews with participants, during the August 1 inspection, the Sperry operator stopped to confirm a rail defect at a point immediately west of the identified point of derailment for this accident, milepost PC 29.26. He marked the defect in the presence of the NS assistant track supervisor. The NS assistant track supervisor told Safety Board investigators that the operator hand inspected within about 2 feet on either side of a defect indication to verify the defect's location. He said he did not recall if the rail in the derailment area exhibited shelling and wear.

A track repair crew, which included the local NS track supervisor, was following the inspection vehicle. The crew repaired the defective rail by cutting out a 42-foot-long rail section that included the defect and installing a replacement rail plug of the same length. The track supervisor said his intention was to remove rail that contained shop welds and some of the rail that had shelling. The east end of this plug abutted the rail segment that failed in this accident. The replacement rail was held in place with bolted joint bars until the joints could be field welded, which occurred on October 10, 2006.

A review of the data from the August 1, 2006, inspection for internal rail defects showed an intermittent loss of bottom signal as the inspection vehicle moved over about a 9-foot length of track 1 in the area of the derailment. The longest continuous loss encompassed about 7 inches of track. Sperry representatives told Safety Board investigators that the shelling on the rail head surface of the recovered rail from the area of the derailment would have interfered with the ultrasonic signal returning from the base of the rail, causing an intermittent loss of bottom signal. A review of the data showed that the location of the largest defect was within a 2-inch area that had a loss of bottom signal in the August 1, 2006, inspection data.

The Sperry operator stated that he did not stop the inspection vehicle to conduct a reinspection or to hand inspect the rails in the area of the intermittent loss of signal because the area of continuous loss was less than 5 feet and thus did not, according to NS instructions, require reinspection.

Rail Inspection Requirements

The FRA regulations regarding rail inspection are found at 49 CFR 213.237. At 49 CFR 213.237(a) (effective January 1, 1999) the FRA states that a continuous search for internal defects shall be made of all rail in Classes 4 through 5 track, and Class 3 track over which passenger trains operate, at least once every 40 million gross tons (mgt) or once a year, whichever interval is shorter.

The FRA's *Track Safety Standards Compliance Manual* defines "continuous search" as an

> uninterrupted search by whatever technology is being used, so that there are no segments of rail that are not tested. If the test is interrupted (e.g., as a result of rail surface conditions that inhibit the transmission or return of the signal) then the test over that segment of rail is not valid because it was not continuous. Therefore, a non-test is not defined in absolute technical terms. Rather, the provision leaves this determination to the rail test equipment operator who is uniquely qualified on that equipment.

Title 49 CFR 213.237(d) states:

> If the person assigned to operate the rail defect detection equipment being used determines that, due to rail surface conditions, a valid search for internal defects could not be made over a particular length of track, the test on that particular length of track cannot be considered as a search for internal defects under paragraph (a) of this section.

When there is a loss of the internal defect detection signal, paragraph (e) should be adhered to. Title 49 CFR 213.237(e) states:

> If a valid search for internal defects cannot be conducted for reasons described in paragraph (d) of this section, the track owner shall, before the expiration of time or tonnage limits:
>
> (1) Conduct a valid search for internal defects;
>
> (2) Reduce operating speed to a maximum of 25 mph until such time as a valid search for internal defects can be made; or
>
> (3) Remove the rail from service.

The staff director for the FRA Track and Structures Division told the Safety Board that the agency was unaware of the NS procedures allowing for a 5-foot loss of bottom signal during internal rail inspections. He stated that a search for defects that allowed this amount of complete or intermittent loss of bottom signal would not constitute a continuous search for defects as defined by the FRA. He stated that he had conducted a telephone query of other railroads and had found instructions similar to those of the NS concerning loss of bottom signals, with some railroads having a 2-foot exception to the requirement for a continuous inspection.

The Association of American Railroads (AAR) addresses the inspection of rail over which hazardous materials are transported in AAR Circular OT-55-I, "Recommended Railroad Operating Practices for Transportation of Hazardous Materials."[30] Circular OT-55 was initially published on January 4, 1990, and was most recently modified on July 17, 2006 (version "I"). In this version, the AAR addresses increased rail inspections for hazardous materials routes. In its guidance regarding key routes, Circular OT-55-I states the following:

> Main track on 'Key Routes' is [to be] inspected by rail defect detection and track geometry inspection cars or any equivalent level of inspection no less than two times each year; sidings are similarly [to be] inspected no less than one time each year, and main track and sidings will have periodic track inspections that will identify cracks or breaks in joint bars.

Federal Oversight of Track and Rail Inspections

FRA track inspectors conduct visual "spot checks" of actual track conditions in selected areas to determine whether a railroad's track inspectors are accurately assessing track conditions and properly documenting them on the records of visual inspections. An FRA spot-check inspection over the NS main track was last conducted on April 18, 2006. No track defects were noted in the area of the derailment.

The FRA reviews the documentation and reports generated from a railroad's internal rail inspections to determine whether the periodic inspections are in compliance with FRA regulations. A railroad's inspection report must document all locations where a valid inspection was not conducted. FRA inspectors typically verify that the required internal rail inspection frequency is met and any rail defects found are repaired or, if repairs are postponed, protections are put in place as required. The NS's most recent preaccident ultrasonic inspection reports for the track in the derailment area did not identify any locations where a valid internal rail inspection was not conducted, and the FRA took no exceptions to the reports.

Placement of Hazardous Materials Cars in Trains

The NS's operating instructions for handling hazardous materials in trains[31] were effective May 31, 2006, and were incorporated into the NS train operating rules. The NS requires each transportation employee to have a copy of and comply with the instructions.

---

[30] Circular OT-55 has been adopted without reservation by members of the AAR and the American Short Line and Regional Railroad Association for their operations within the United States.

[31] NS *United States Hazardous Materials Instructions for Rail* (HM-1), effective May 31, 2006.

The instructions for handling hazardous materials require the use of "buffer" cars to separate placarded[32] hazardous materials cars from the locomotive units and any other occupied cars for the protection of train crews. NS representatives told the Safety Board that the company's hazardous materials instructions allow a single car to be used as a buffer between a placarded hazardous materials car and the locomotive(s) on unit trains[33] transporting hazardous materials if no additional buffer cars are available on the train. The UP, which delivered the accident train to the NS in Chicago, states in its hazardous materials rules[34] that if five buffer cars are not available to separate the placarded hazardous materials cars from the locomotive unit on a train, all available buffer cars are to be placed between the locomotive unit and the placarded cars, but at least one buffer car is required.

The Pipeline and Hazardous Materials Safety Administration (PHMSA) in the U.S. Department of Transportation (DOT) has the authority to develop and promulgate regulations for the safe transport of hazardous materials in all transportation modes. The regulation governing the use of buffer cars in trains for the protection of the crew is in 49 CFR Part 174, and the FRA has the authority to enforce these regulations. A table at 49 CFR 174.85(d) states, in part:

> 1. When train length permits, [a] placarded car may not be nearer than the sixth car from the engine or occupied caboose.
>
> 2. When train length does not permit, [a] placarded car must be placed near the middle of the train, but not nearer than the second car from an engine or occupied caboose.

The requirements in 49 CFR 174.85 do not specifically address unit trains transporting hazardous materials or otherwise make a distinction between general freight trains, unit trains, and short trains operating between industrial facilities and local rail yards. However, both the FRA and PHMSA have recently issued interpretations of 49 CFR 174.85 regarding unit trains.

In a January 31, 2006, letter, the FRA responded to a petition filed on behalf of the United Transportation Union. The union had challenged another major railroad's practice of using a one-car buffer on its ethanol unit trains as a violation of the DOT Hazardous Materials Regulations. In its response, the FRA stated the following:

> If a train is made up of all hazardous materials cars, like a unit train of ethanol tank cars, this requirement may be met by a single buffer car separating the locomotive from the hazardous materials cars.

---

[32] *Placards* are signs affixed to railroad freight cars, highway trailers and tanks, and intermodal freight containers to signify that the car, trailer, or container is carrying hazardous materials. The placards are color-coded and bear numbers that identify the specific hazardous material being carried and its hazards.

[33] A unit train is a freight train in which all cars carry the same commodity and are bound for the same destination.

[34] *UP Instructions for Handling Hazardous Materials*, Form 8620, dated April 6, 2003.

The director of PHMSA's Office of Hazardous Materials Standards, in a March 29, 2007, letter in response to a Safety Board inquiry regarding specific buffer car requirements for unit trains containing only placarded hazardous materials cars, stated that the requirement to place placarded cars no nearer than the sixth car from the engine or occupied caboose

> applies so long as there are sufficient non-hazardous materials rail cars within the standing train consist to fulfill the requirement. The regulations do not require railroads to change business or operating decisions concerning the number and types of cars placed in the train.

The letter added that when the number of nonhazardous cars within a train is insufficient to provide a five-car buffer, at least one buffer car should be placed between the loaded placarded cars and the locomotives.

In June 2005, the FRA submitted a report to Congress — *Safe Placement of Train Cars* — in response to a mandate under the Hazardous Materials Transportation Authorization Act of 1994 (Public Law 103-311). The Secretary of the DOT was asked to conduct a study of

> two related, but distinct, issues: first, the make-up of trains in such a manner as to prevent derailments caused by in-train forces and, second, placement of hazardous materials cars in trains so as to avoid harm to crew members or interaction of hazardous materials, should a train accident or other unintended release occur.

The report also contained a brief history of the development and evolution of the car placement standards for crew protection that are found in 49 CFR 174.85(d). According to the report, just after the turn of the 20th century Congress directed the Interstate Commerce Commission to

> formulate and publish "Regulations For The Transportation of Explosives" to promote the safe transportation in interstate commerce of explosives and other dangerous articles.

The FRA report further noted that the impetus for the early laws and regulations was due to the number of accidents involving the transportation of explosive black powder. The early regulations required cars with explosives to be placed near the center of the train and at least 16 cars from the engine and 10 cars from the caboose when the length of the train would permit. The standard of a 16-car buffer was selected because it was considered to be a safe distance to prevent cinders from steam locomotives from reaching wooden box cars containing explosives. By 1922, new regulations were in effect that required a five-car separation between placarded cars transporting flammable materials and either a locomotive or an occupied caboose. When the length of the train did not permit, the car transporting the hazardous materials was to be placed in the middle of the train and separated from the engine or caboose by at least one car.

The report also noted that the current in-train placement requirements are founded "on no more rigorous a scientific basis than were the original [requirements]." The FRA emphasized that the current requirements are based on the "empirical evidence of history" and that there is no body of evidence from the analysis of accident data to support the need for "sudden or drastic overhaul" of these requirements.

The FRA noted in the report that Canada and the United Kingdom also have evaluated the effectiveness of buffer cars and the placement of placarded hazardous materials cars in trains for the protection of train crews. Although the Canadian regulations are similar to the DOT Hazardous Materials Regulations, they do not require buffer cars in unit trains transporting hazardous materials. Canadian regulations do require a five-car separation between cars carrying flammable gases and loaded tank cars transporting chlorine, anhydrous ammonia, or sulfur dioxide, all of which are either toxic by inhalation or designated inhalation hazards. British regulations do not require a buffer car between occupied rail cars and cars transporting hazardous materials. However, in its report the FRA did note that British regulations tend to be more restrictive regarding chemical compatibility requirements.

The FRA concluded in its 2005 report that

> Existing regulations regarding train placement of hazardous materials have been fashioned through long experience and have functioned well. The requirement that tank cars carrying hazardous materials be placed at least six deep provides suitable protection for train crews without creating excessive issues regarding train make-up (e.g., location of loaded cars). … Existing in-train placement requirements appear to provide for an appropriate level of safety.

The 2005 report did not otherwise address the risks specifically associated with a one-car buffer on unit trains transporting hazardous materials.

Hazardous Materials Information

Ethanol Shipments by Rail

Natural gasoline[35] was used to denature the ethanol carried in the accident train. According to the Ethanol Product Materials Safety Data Sheet, the components of the blend of denatured ethanol on the accident train were ethyl alcohol (95.0 percent), natural gasoline (5.0 percent), and benzene (less than 0.25 percent). Denatured ethanol is a flammable liquid with a flash point near 49° F. It burns without a visible flame in daylight. It is a clean, colorless liquid with a

---

[35] *Natural gasoline* is gasoline that is extracted from natural gas rather than produced at an oil refinery.

characteristic odor; it is lighter than water and soluble in water. Its vapors are heavier than air, and it is used as a fuel, solvent, anti-freeze, and to make other chemicals. Denatured ethanol is regulated by the DOT as "alcohols N.O.S., Class 3–flammable liquid."

According to the AAR, the number of annual rail shipments of denatured alcohol/ethanol increased from 33,288 to 76,734 between 2000 and 2005. The growing demand for ethanol is largely due to the increasing use of ethanol as an additive to automotive gasoline.

Tests and Research

Examination of Recovered Rail

About 19 feet of broken rail (five pieces varying in length from 13.75 to 60.5 inches and two small pieces) from the accident area were recovered and transported to the Safety Board's Materials Laboratory for examination. The rail pieces came from the north rail (left rail in direction of train movement) and included the rail from the identified point of derailment. Initial examination and measurement revealed that a rail piece about 64 inches long had not been recovered. The total length represented by the recovered rail was thus about 24 feet 4 1/2 inches. The rail pieces were laid out and matched to determine their original placement, as shown in figure 5.

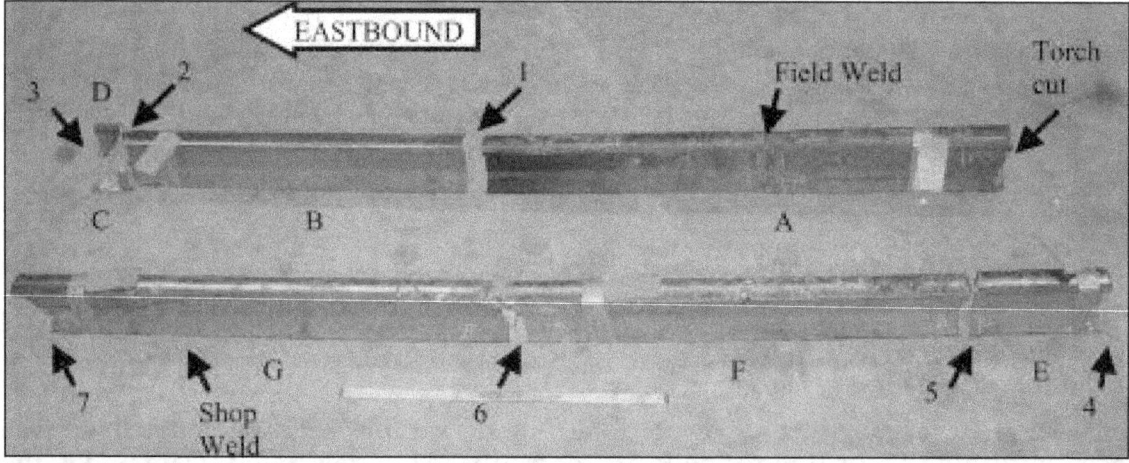

Figure 5. Field side of recovered rail after reassembly. (The rail pieces are lettered west to east; fractures are numbered west to east. The missing 64-inch-long rail section is bounded by fractures 3 and 4.)

Shell flakes, spalling, and open shell cracks were present along the length of recovered rail. The rail contained seven complete fractures (through the rail head, web, and base), which are numbered 1 through 7 in figure 5. Six of the seven fracture faces contained transverse defects encompassing from 8 to 78 percent of the worn rail head area. All the defects showed features consistent with a detail fracture from shelling, with several fractures emanating from an open shell crack at the gage corner. The largest defect, covering 78 percent of the worn rail head, was found at fracture 4. The second largest defect, covering 45 percent of the worn rail head, was at fracture 5. Both fracture surfaces showed features consistent with detail fracture from shelling. (See figure 6.)

Figure 6. View of east surface of fracture 4. (The dashed line indicates the boundary of a detail fracture covering about 78 percent of the worn rail head and extending into the web. The defect emanated from an open shell crack at the gage corner.)

Fractures 4 and 5 were at each end of a 14-inch-long piece of rail. This piece had receiving rail-end batter at fracture 4, and the other end of this piece had no trailing batter at fracture 5. The mating piece of recovered rail had a relatively small amount of receiving batter at fracture 5.

Ultrasonic Inspection of Recovered Rail

The five larger recovered rail pieces were inspected using handheld ultrasonic inspection equipment. Inspection began with a 0° transducer for a signal reflection from the bottom of the rail at the center of the running surface. Next, a 70° transducer was used to check for indications of transverse defects by scanning in both directions longitudinally along the rail surface at the center, gage, and field sides and along the sides of the head at the field and gage sides.[36]

---

[36] Several areas of the rail had open spall cracks in the gage side of the head, preventing these areas from being inspected using the handheld equipment. Also, the narrow width of the rail head on the gage side sometimes made it difficult for the standard-size transducer to maintain proper contact with the rail surface.

Except for some small sections on one rail piece and at other areas of known interference (such as welds and joint bar holes), a bottom signal was received throughout the entire length of the rail pieces. Inspection of the rail from the running surface using the 70° transducer identified an indication of a potential flaw on the gage side near the running surface. Inspection of the rail from the gage side of the rail head with the same transducer resulted in six indications of potential defects at five locations.

At each of the six locations where the ultrasound inspection had indicated a possible defect, Safety Board investigators cut and then fractured the rail. Four of the fractures had uniform rough gray features consistent with overstress fracture with no indications of transverse defects intersecting the lab fracture surface. A portion of the surface of one lab fracture had features consistent with a defect that had not opened to the surface. This defect covered about 5 percent of the worn rail head area. Two areas of the surface in another lab fracture had features consistent with a pair of transverse defects in proximity to one another. These combined defects covered less than 5 percent of the remaining head area. A shell crack that was oriented almost parallel to the gage corner was observed at the inner boundary of the detail fracture areas, and the fracture features radiated outward toward the surface from the intersection with the shell crack. None of the transverse defects that were found at the lab fracture locations had been indicated during the lab's inspection using the 70° transducer from the running surface of the rail.

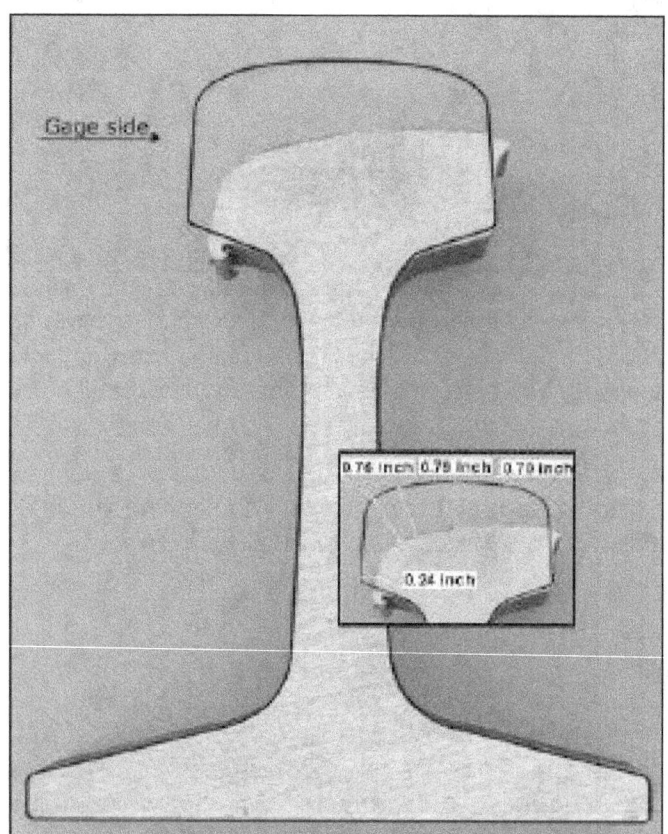

Figure 7. Cross section of one of the recovered rail pieces examined in the Safety Board's Materials Laboratory. (Superimposed on the rail is a profile of new 140-pound rail. The inset image shows the amount of head loss since rail was new.)

Rail Profile Measurements

Figure 7 superimposes the outline of a new 140-pound rail onto a photograph of a transverse section of rail from the derailment area. As shown, the vertical head loss at the center of the head was 0.70 inch. Measuring radially inward, the loss from the gage corner was 0.76 to 0.79 inch. At the lower end of the gage side of the head, the loss in the horizontal direction was 0.24 inch. About 40 percent of the head area had been worn away or removed by a combination of wear and rail grinding. The lower edge of the rail head on both the gage and the field sides also extended below the profile, which is consistent with the overall downward deformation of a worn head under wheel loads.

NS standards allow rail head (top-vertical) wear of 11/16 (0.6875) inch for 140-pound rail in main line service with accumulated tonnage of more than 5 mgt before the rail is recommended for replacement, that is, listed for future replacement. If vertical wear exceeds 13/16 (0.8125) inch, trains are to be put under a slow order until the rail is replaced. An NS chief engineer stated that the NS standard for 140-pound rails allows 1/2 (0.5) inch of gage face wear before the rail is recommended for replacement. If gage face wear exceeds 10/16 (0.6250) inch, trains are put under a slow order until the rail is replaced.

Measurements of vertical head loss of the rail pieces examined in the Safety Board's Materials Laboratory showed rail head losses ranging from 0.38 to 0.70 inch. When measured with a rail wear template of the type that railroads used to evaluate rail wear, the vertical head loss was indicated to be about 1/8 (0.1625) inch less than the actual loss.

Transverse Defect Growth Rate

Studies by the DOT[37] have shown that the primary factor in the rate of crack growth from internal defects in rail is the traffic load. Influences on the rate of transverse defect growth in rail include bending stresses applied to the rail during train operations and sudden or large temperature variations. Temperature changes can place rail under tension or compression, making internal flaws more susceptible to growth. Bending stresses from heavy-axle-load traffic make these defects even more susceptible to fatigue damage and progression. Traffic load is the primary factor in producing stress cycles for crack growth in rail.

Sperry calculated the anticipated normal growth rate of detail fractures in rail as 1.6 to 2.0 percent of the cross section of the head of new rail[38] with every 1 mgt of traffic. Based on the estimated traffic load and calculated growth rate, Sperry calculated that detail fractures found in the rail at the point of derailment likely would have progressed about 20 percent (for a new rail head) between the latest inspection and the accident. According to Sperry representatives, the internal transverse rail flaws were at or below borderline detection size at the time

---

[37] (a) D.Y. Jeong, T.H. Tang, O. Orringer, and A.B. Perlman, *Propagation Analysis of Transverse Defects Originating at the Lower Gage Corner of Rail*, U.S. Department of Transportation, DOT/FRA/ORD-98/06 (1998). (b) D.Y. Jeong, *Analytical Modeling of Rail Defects and Its Applications to Rail Defect Management*, U.S. Department of Transportation, Research and Special Programs Administration, Volpe National Transportation Systems Center (2003).

[38] Standard industry practice is to define defect size as a percentage of the cross-sectional area of the rail head of a new rail.

of the August 1 inspection, leading Sperry to assign "growth" as the reason for nondetection.

The largest defect found in the accident rail recovered from the accident site encompassed about 78 percent of the worn rail head. The area of the defect on the worn accident rail head equates to a defect size of 47 percent of a new rail head. The likely size of this fracture at the time of the most recent ultrasonic inspection, on August 1, was calculated by the DOT's Volpe National Transportation Systems Center using its analytical model for transverse defect growth. The variables entered into the calculation included 140-pound rail on a 0.8° curve in Class 4 track, a critical crack size of 47 percent, vertical head loss of 0.7 inch, gage face loss of 0.24 inch, and an accumulated tonnage of 14 mgt. Using this data, the estimated size of the defect at the time of the last inspection was between 8 and 14 percent of a new rail head.

In the absence of precise data on temperature differential[39] and average wheel loads, a range of values was used. In each case, higher values for temperature differential or average wheel loads or both resulted in faster transverse defect growth rates and correspondingly smaller estimated defect sizes at last inspection.

The DOT studies previously referenced have shown that detail fractures grow faster in worn rail and the critical size for failure is lower. In the 1998 study that analyzed transverse defect growth, calculations showed that for 132-pound rail on a 5° curve with a Class 3 or 4 level of foundation stiffness and no thermal loads, a defect grows from 10 percent of the rail head to a critical size of more than 80 percent of the head area after about 55 mgt has moved over it. Under the same conditions but in rail with a 40-percent vertical head loss, the defect grows from 10 percent to a critical size of 25 percent after carrying 7.5 mgt. Under baseline conditions of a 15° F temperature differential and an average wheel load of 16,500 pounds (baseline values from Jeong, 2003), a transverse defect in 140-pound rail at the NS's established rail wear standard could grow from 11 to 12 percent to critical size within 14 mgt of traffic load.

Derailments Caused by Broken Rail

According to data compiled by the FRA, 158 main track derailments caused by broken rail occurred in 2006, resulting in about $65 million in damages. The most frequently cited cause (35 incidents) was "transverse/compound fissures broken rails." The second leading cause (25 incidents) was "shelling/head checks broken rails." In 2005, "shelling/head checks broken rails" was also the second leading cause of derailments (35 incidents), just ahead of "transverse/compound fissures broken rails" (33 incidents).

---

[39] *Temperature differential* refers to the difference between the rail's *neutral* temperature (the temperature at which the rail is under neither tension nor compression) and its actual temperature.

Other Information

NS Postaccident Actions

On October 19, 2007, the NS issued a memorandum to Sperry with the subject "Testing Critical and Open Deck Bridges." The memorandum provided instruction for use by all NS-assigned detector cars when inspecting track on "critical and open deck bridges along with bridges over navigable waterways." Attached to and referenced by the memorandum is *MW&S* [Maintenance of Way and Structures] *Standard Procedure No. 030*: "Instructions for Inspection of Bridges, Culverts, and Tunnels." The memorandum includes the following instructions:

- Test speed shall not exceed 5 mph.
- Any equipment response generated by the test system within 234 feet of either side of bridge must be acknowledged with an icon or supporting remarks representing the operator's interpretation.
- Any equipment response typical to a fillet or weld reflector[40] must be confirmed visually by the operator.
- All suspect equipment responses must be hand tested and verified that a defective condition is not present.
- Extra care should be taken with surface conditions and/or any unexplained 'Loss of Bottom' [signal] that may prevent the detection of an underlying defect. All such indications must be ground examined and hand tested. Any surface condition that prevents a valid test must be reported as a Rail Test Exception governed by FRA Track Safety Standard 213.237(d).

NS representatives told investigators that because the railroad's Beaver River bridge spans a navigable waterway, it would be covered by the new instructions.

FRA Postaccident Actions

In an effort to help reduce the number of derailments caused by broken rails, the FRA is in the process of establishing a Rail Integrity Section within its Track and Structures Division. The responsibilities of this group will include reviewing railroads' rail-inspection procedures, auditing railroads' rail-inspection requirements, developing new information to be used in rail inspection, and investigating broken-rail derailments, including reviewing rail inspection reports for the derailment area. The FRA has informed the Safety Board that it hired a manager for the Track and Structures Division in March 2008 and is currently seeking to hire eight regional rail integrity specialists.

---

40 *Fillets* and *weld deflectors* are not rail defects.

Beaver County Postaccident Actions

In September 2007, Beaver County Emergency Services, along with emergency services in 13 other counties, participated in the Southwest Pennsylvania Region 13 annual emergency-response group exercise. The NS participated in the Beaver County portion of the exercise. The exercise involved a tank car leak/release and focused on testing crisis management, communication, incident command, and entry into a rail yard.

NS Disaster Preparedness

On February 17, 2006, NS hazardous materials personnel held a security awareness event at Conway yard for local firefighters and police officers. About 33 people attended. On September 5, 2002, the NS participated in a full-scale drill with Allegheny County.

One month before the accident, on September 20, 2006, the NS hosted the Transcaer[41] Whistle-Stop event in Pittsburgh. About 222 individuals attended the event, including the Beaver County director of emergency services (the incident commander for the accident) and the director of Allegheny County Emergency Services.

The NS also provides funding for local emergency responders to attend the Emergency Response Training Center in Pueblo, Colorado. The Center has a 1-week course that includes hands-on training, mock derailments, and exercises. In recent years, participants have included the Beaver County director of emergency services, a representative of Allegheny County Emergency Services, a representative of the Pittsburgh Fire Department, a representative of the Washington County Hazardous Materials Team, and a representative of the Big Beaver Volunteer Fire Department. In 2007, the NS invited personnel from the New Brighton Fire Department, the Pittsburgh Fire Department, Allegheny County, and the Beaver County Emergency Services Center to participate in training at the Emergency Response Training Center.

Previous Safety Board Action Regarding Internal Rail Inspections

In its investigation of a June 30, 1992, derailment of a Burlington Northern freight train on an approach to a bridge in Superior, Wisconsin,[42] which resulted in a hazardous materials release and the evacuation of more than 40,000 people,

---

[41] Transportation Community Awareness and Emergency Response (Transcaer), is a voluntary national outreach effort to help communities prepare for and respond to a hazardous materials transportation incident. Transcaer is sponsored by the AAR, the American Chemistry Council, Chemical Educational Foundation, CHEMTREC®, the Chlorine Institute, Inc., and National Tank Truck Carriers, Inc.

[42] National Transportation Safety Board, *Derailment of Burlington Northern Freight Train No. 01-142-30 and Release of Hazardous Materials in the Town of Superior, Wisconsin, June 30, 1992.* Railroad/Hazardous Materials Accident Report NTSB/HZM-94-01 (Washington, DC: NTSB 1994).

the Safety Board identified a safety issue involving ultrasonic rail inspections. The investigation determined that an undetected internal rail defect (a detail fracture) caused the rail to break and derail the train.

The broken rail had been ultrasonically inspected about 1 month before the accident. The ultrasonic rail equipment operator had observed fluctuations in the initial inspection readings, but after repeated inspection, both with the rail-car-mounted ultrasonic equipment and with handheld equipment, he had recorded the inspection results as "marginal to satisfactory" because of the age of the rail and the rail surface conditions that interfered with signal penetration. As a result of its investigation of the accident, the Safety Board, on April 1, 1994, issued the following safety recommendations:

To the FRA:

R-94-1
Research and develop, with the assistance of the Association of American Railroads, inspection methods that will identify internal defects in rail that has significant shelling and other surface conditions.

R-94-2
Perform the necessary research and develop standards that (1) provide defined limits of allowable rail surface conditions (such as shelling) that can hinder the identification of internal defects, and (2) require remedial action for rail with surface conditions that exceed defined limits.

To the AAR:

R-94-4
Assist the Federal Railroad Administration in researching and developing inspection methods that will identify internal defects in rail that has shelling and other surface conditions.

R-94-5
Assist the Federal Railroad Administration in correlating rail surface conditions with detail fractures and with rail service failures, including the provision of samples of rail with detail fractures.

In a February 8, 1996, letter in response to Safety Recommendation R-94-1, the FRA stated that the recommended research was unnecessary because the industry was already performing similar efforts. The same FRA letter responded to R-94-2 stating that the chances of producing a useful outcome from such a research effort were doubtful and that no research was planned in this area. Because the FRA did not express a willingness to sponsor or encourage research and development of new inspection methods capable of identifying internal defects in rail with significant head surface conditions, the Safety Board, on April 9, 1996, classified Safety Recommendations R-94-1 and -2 "Closed—Unacceptable Action."

In a December 9, 1997, letter in response to Safety Recommendation R-94-4, the AAR informed the Safety Board that a joint FRA-AAR project was underway to conduct research and to develop inspection methods to identify defects in rail that has shelling or other surface defects. Based on this response, the Board classified Safety Recommendation R-94-4 "Closed—Acceptable Action" on May 14, 1998.

Although the FRA had not responded favorably to its two safety recommendations arising from the Superior, Wisconsin, accident investigation, the AAR informed the Safety Board in a January 14, 2002, letter that the AAR and its member railroads had worked with the FRA through the FRA's Rail Safety Advisory Committee (RSAC) process to implement new provisions in the FRA Track Safety Standards. These new provisions became effective in September 1998. The new provisions that were made as a result of the Safety Board's safety recommendations developed during the Superior, Wisconsin, accident investigation were implemented through paragraphs (d) and (e) of 49 CFR 213.237 of the Track Safety Standards (provided earlier in this report). Because these changes were responsive to the Board's concerns, the Board, on May 2, 2002, classified Safety Recommendation R-94-5 "Closed—Acceptable Alternate Action."[43]

---

[43] Although the AAR advised the Safety Board that the FRA had participated through the RSAC process to revise the Track Safety Standards to address Safety Recommendations R-94-1 and -2, because of the FRA's lack a of timely positive response to the recommendations and its failure to inform the Board that it had addressed the intent of recommendations, the classification of those safety recommendations remains "Closed—Unacceptable Action."

ANALYSIS

Exclusions

The investigation determined that the engineer and conductor of NS train 68QB119 were qualified employees who had been trained and tested in the proper performance of their duties. The work and rest histories of the two crewmembers did not indicate that either of them was suffering from fatigue before or at the time of the accident. Postaccident toxicological tests were negative for the presence of alcohol as well as FRA-specified drugs. The crew stated that they had not noted any irregularities or problems with the train between Toledo and the point of the derailment, and investigators found nothing unusual in the crewmembers' handling of the train. The Safety Board therefore concludes that the following were not factors in the accident: crewmembers' qualifications, fatigue, drugs or alcohol, and the crewmembers' operation of the train.

A review of preaccident equipment mechanical inspections, data from wayside defect detectors, and train crew statements did not reveal anything unusual. Postaccident equipment inspections found no defective equipment on the train. All wheel impact readings for the accident train were within normal limits as specified by the NS. The Safety Board concludes that the mechanical condition of the train was not a factor in the derailment.

The NS provided timely and accurate information about the train consist to local emergency responders, identifying denatured ethanol as the only hazardous materials product involved in the derailment. The investigation found that the incident command system worked well, with railroad personnel available to assist in coordination. The Safety Board concludes that the emergency response and the command system were effective and appropriate.

The Accident

Postaccident inspection by Safety Board investigators found pieces of broken rail under the last derailed car. When, as in this instance, a rail completely breaks (through the rail head, web, and base) and separates, the electrical circuit continuity in the track signal system may be interrupted, causing the most restrictive signal indication to be displayed to the locomotive. The engineer of the accident train stated, and signal system data confirmed, that the train was operated on a *clear* signal indication over the bridge. After the locomotive left the east end of the NS bridge over the Beaver River and traveled about 200 yards, the cab signal indication went from *clear* to *approach*, as the train entered another track circuit.

Shortly afterward, as the rest of the train was crossing the bridge, the train brakes went into an emergency application because of the rail separation and derailment. The Safety Board concludes that the derailment occurred when the north rail of track 1 separated under the load of the accident train.

Rail Defects and Ultrasonic Inspection

During the examination of seven pieces of broken rail recovered from the accident scene, the Safety Board's Materials Laboratory found pre-existing transverse defects (fatigue cracks) at the site of breaks in the north rail of track 1, as well as at other locations within the unbroken rail segments. All the transverse defects found in the rail, including the defect at the primary fracture, were identified as detail fractures from shelling.

The largest defect size was at fracture 4; it covered about 78 percent of the existing worn rail head. The next largest defect size was at fracture 5, which covered about 45 percent of the rail head. These two fractures were at the ends of a 14-inch-long piece of rail. Rail-end batter patterns observed at the fractured ends of the recovered pieces indicated that the rail initially broke at fracture 4. Therefore, the primary rail break occurred at the location of the largest defect, with the other fractures secondary to the initial separation. The Safety Board concludes that the failure of the north rail of track 1 was precipitated by a detail fracture (fatigue crack) that originated from shelling on the rail head, reached critical size, and caused a piece of rail to break out under the train.

The rail had been inspected for internal defects about 2 1/2 months before the accident using an instrumented vehicle. At that time, the vehicle operator did not identify any internal rail defects in these sections of rail. The investigation determined that the site of the rail failure was within a 9-foot length of rail where, because of rail surface conditions, the ultrasonic inspection equipment had received only intermittent signal returns from the bottom of the rail.

Based on defect (crack) growth calculations, at the time of the August 1, 2006, rail inspection, the size of the largest defect, which initiated the rail fracture, would likely have been approximately 8 to 14 percent of a new rail head area.[44] Based on Safety Board laboratory evaluations and the TTCI data in table 1, the size of the initiating defect was likely too small[45] at that time to be reliably detected. Also, the shelling that was evident on the rail surface as well as the crack patterns from flaking that were observed on a cross section of the accident rail could have prevented ultrasonic signals sent from the running surface from detecting

---

[44] Defect size is typically given as a percentage of the rail head area of a new rail. The area of the largest defect at the time of the August 1 rail inspection would likely have covered approximately 13 to 23 percent of the existing worn rail head.

[45] The TTCI data estimates a 64-percent probability of detection for a defect size of 8 percent of the rail head using an inspection vehicle.

the defect. A correlation of the data from the August 1, 2006, inspection with the locations of the recovered rail from the area of the derailment showed that the location of the initiating defect was within a 2-inch area that had a loss of bottom signal. The Safety Board therefore concludes that rail surface conditions prevented the effective transmission of the ultrasonic signals, and the defect (fatigue crack) that led to the derailment may not have been large enough at that time to be reliably detected by the inspection vehicle.

FRA regulations require that all railroads conduct a "continuous search" when inspecting rail for internal defects. In the FRA's interpretation of the regulations, any rail inspection that is interrupted "as a result of rail surface conditions that inhibit the transmission or return of the signal" is not considered to be continuous under the regulation and therefore is not to be considered a valid inspection of the affected rail segment.

About a year and a half before the accident and without consulting the FRA, the NS gave its inspection contractor (Sperry) new procedures for inspecting rail for internal defects. In effect, the new procedures permitted the equipment operator to ignore any loss of bottom signal as long as the continuous loss-of-signal distance did not exceed 5 feet of linear rail length. The new procedures were intended to address the detection of vertically oriented longitudinal rail head defects, not transverse defects. Although the new procedures were designed to address a different type of defect, the procedures were applied to the entire inspection process and thereby also affected the detection of transverse defects.

The point of derailment was within a rail segment about 9 feet long where, during the August 1 ultrasonic inspection, the inspection equipment had encountered an intermittent loss of bottom signal. Because the longest loss of bottom signal distance was only about 7 inches of linear rail length (which did not exceed the 5-foot minimum specified by the NS that would have required a repeat inspection), this rail segment was not examined further.

The flaking and shelling conditions found on the recovered rail head likely blocked the ultrasonic signals at several locations and caused the intermittent loss of bottom signal at the point of derailment. Because the NS did not require the contractor to repeat the inspection of the rail at these locations, the area was not examined further by Sperry, and the internal condition of the rail at these locations was left undetermined. The NS exception to the continuous search requirement eliminated an opportunity to detect the defect that led to the derailment by rerunning the inspection vehicle or by using more effective handheld inspection equipment.

Reinspection of a rail segment having a loss of bottom signal usually entails a handheld scan in which the inspector runs a handheld transducer across the running surface of the rail. Handheld scans can be more effective than inspection vehicles, but data are not available on the probability of detection for handheld inspections at a range of defect sizes. In tests conducted in the Safety Board's

Materials Laboratory, handheld scans of segments of rail showed that two rail head internal defects having a size of 3 percent[46] or less were not detected by hand inspections at the running surface of the rail head. (These defects were found using a laboratory technique that scans the side of the rail head.) The estimated defect size at the time of the last inspection before the accident was only slightly larger than the defects found using the laboratory technique. Even if the Sperry equipment operator had used a handheld scanning device to inspect the rail where the bottom signal was intermittently lost during his inspection on August 1, he still may not have found the defect that led to the rail fracture. Therefore, it could not be determined whether the defect that led to the rail fracture would have been found had a handheld inspection device been used to reinspect the area that had the loss of bottom signal on August 1, 2006.

Exempting any length of rail from a valid inspection could result in missing a defect that could grow to critical size before the next inspection and lead to rail failure under the load of a train. The Safety Board concludes that NS procedures that do not require a re-examination of rail where there is a signal loss during ultrasonic inspection means that those segments of rail can remain uninspected and in service indefinitely. Therefore, the Safety Board believes that the NS should revise its ultrasonic rail inspection procedures to eliminate exceptions to the requirement for an uninterrupted, continuous search for rail defects.

The Safety Board issued recommendations that addressed the effectiveness of internal rail inspections as a result of its investigation of the Burlington Northern freight train accident that occurred in Superior, Wisconsin, in 1992. New provisions were added to the Track Safety Standards through paragraphs (d) and (e) of 49 CFR 213.237 that were responsive to the Board's recommendations. These provisions appear to ensure that railroads are required to conduct valid continuous searches for internal defects and that no segments of rail are to remain in service without being inspected.

The FRA reviews the documentation and reports generated from a railroad's internal rail inspections to determine whether the required inspection frequency is met and that any rail defects found are repaired or, if repairs are postponed, protections are put in place as required. These reviews are an important part of the FRA's oversight responsibilities to identify potential safety deficiencies on the railroad. However, the investigation found that the NS procedures allowed as much as 5 continuous feet of signal loss during its ultrasonic inspections, which is not consistent with the requirement in the Track Safety Standards for a continuous search. The NS's preaccident ultrasonic inspection reports for the rail in the derailment area did not identify locations where a valid inspection was not conducted, even though a 9-foot length of track in the area of the derailment showed an intermittent loss of signal. Further, the FRA was not aware that the NS and other railroads had enacted various exceptions to the requirement for a continuous search. The FRA's reviews of railroad rail inspection programs should

---

[46] Defect size is stated as a percentage of rail head area of a new rail head.

have identified these inconsistencies. The Safety Board concludes that the FRA's oversight of the NS's and other railroads' internal rail inspection processes was inadequate. Although the Board notes that the FRA is in the process of establishing a rail integrity group that will examine railroads' internal rail inspection programs, the Board understands that the FRA has not required that railroads eliminate potential exceptions to the requirement for a continuous search. The Safety Board believes that the FRA should review all railroads' internal rail defect detection procedures and require changes to those procedures as necessary to eliminate exceptions to the requirement for an uninterrupted, continuous search for rail defects.

Rail Defect Management

The rail in the accident area had been in service at this location since 1977. No records were found to indicate the total gross tonnage over the track since that time, but because this track was a main east-west line for the predecessor railroads (Pennsylvania, Penn Central, and Conrail) as well as the NS, it could reasonably be estimated to have carried in excess of 1 billion gross tons (1,000 mgt) before the derailment. Most railroads measure rail wear and consider those wear levels when scheduling rail for replacement. Measurements taken after the accident showed that the rail in some locations in the accident area was near or exceeded the wear level at which the NS would list the rail to be replaced. However, the wear on the rail had not yet reached the level at which the NS would implement a speed restriction.

Over the years, transverse defects have been among the leading causes of train derailments on Class 3, 4, and 5 track.[47] To find defects that can lead to derailments, the FRA Track Safety Standards require that a continuous search for internal rail defects be made for Classes 4 and 5 track (and Class 3 track over which passenger trains operate) after every 40 mgt of traffic or once a year, whichever interval is shorter. The interval between inspections is intended to provide a safe time frame for detection of internal rail flaws before they can grow to critical size and cause a rail break.

To reduce the risk that an ultrasonic inspection will miss a rail defect that will later become critical, some railroads have developed databases to capture information on track conditions, train activities, and rail defects found by inspection or in-service fractures. These railroads use this information to monitor rail conditions and predict future performance. The NS based its ultrasonic rail inspection schedule on a model that takes into account track speed, annual tonnage, hazardous materials transported over the route, whether the territory is signaled or nonsignaled, rail weight and age, curvature, and rail defect/failure history. Rail head wear is not a parameter in the model. Using this model, the NS determined

---

[47] FRA database: Rail, Joint Bar, and Rail Anchoring Derailments, for all railroads, on main track.

that the track in the accident area should be inspected with ultrasound equipment four times per year.

NS records indicated that track 1 carried about 63.5 mgt per year. Therefore, ultrasonic inspections of this track four times per year resulted in an average interval of about 16 mgt, which was well within the 40-mgt maximum established by the FRA. However, one of a number of factors that can influence growth rates of transverse defects in rail is the amount of rail head wear. When a rail has less material to support the load it carries, the stress levels are higher, which leads to higher crack growth rates and reduced tolerance for a given crack size. Studies conducted by the DOT's Volpe Center have confirmed that detail fractures grow faster in worn rail than in new rail, and the critical crack size for failure is smaller.

For worn rail, the time a defect takes to grow from undetectable to critical size is shorter, which increases the risk of failure between inspections. The rail at the point of derailment showed a loss of 40 percent of the rail head area from wear and grinding. Calculations indicate that in the area of the accident, a defect size of 8 to 14 percent[48] at the time of the August 1 inspection grew to critical size after passage of about 13.8 mgt of traffic, which was less than the average 16 mgt inspection interval developed by the NS. The Safety Board concludes that the NS did not conduct internal rail inspections frequently enough to reliably detect an internal defect before it could grow to critical size in the significantly worn rail.

The New Brighton accident illustrates that as rail wears, it requires more frequent inspections to detect internal defects before they can reach critical size and cause a failure. A defect that was too small to be reliably detected during an internal inspection grew to critical size between inspections even when the interval was more frequent than the 40-mgt or at-least-once-per-year interval required by the FRA. The Safety Board concludes that the FRA's required minimum intervals for internal rail inspections are inadequate because they do not take into account the effect of rail wear, which can allow undetected internal rail defects to grow to critical size between required inspections.

The degree of wear on the accident rail was a factor in the rapid progression of the defect from small to critical size. One of the issues highlighted by the circumstances of this accident is the inadequacy of the internal rail inspection requirement based solely on time and tonnage as set forth in Federal regulations, rather than a damage-tolerance approach.

A damage-tolerance approach would establish an inspection frequency that allows internal rail defects to be identified before they reach critical size. The term *damage tolerance* means the ability of a structure to withstand damage without failure, including damage such as fatigue cracking or wear, which can develop from undetected manufacturing defects or from use in service. For most

---

[48] Defect size is stated as a percentage of rail head area of a new rail head.

engineered structural components, including rail, an inspection and maintenance program to detect and repair damage in any component before it reaches critical size is integral to the damage tolerance of the structure. A damage-tolerance approach should (1) identify areas of rail that are prone to failure from high stress and fatigue and (2) determine appropriate inspection intervals based on the defect size detectable by the inspection method being used, the stress level, and the defect (crack) propagation characteristics in the structure. Such an approach would consider all the factors that can affect defect growth rates, including rail head wear, accumulated tonnage, rail surface conditions, track geometry, track support, steel specifications, temperature differentials, and residual stresses in the rail. The capabilities and limitations of the inspection methods used to detect defects are a major factor in determining appropriate inspection intervals in a damage-tolerance approach.

Each railroad should have a rail inspection and maintenance program that addresses its unique operating environment and the effectiveness of its inspection methods. As noted previously, the NS had established rail wear standards, but the amount of wear on the accident rail was sufficient to facilitate rapid progression of a relatively small defect. The Safety Board concludes that, in the absence of a damage-tolerance-based program, rail can remain in use with excessive accumulated wear, which increases the risk of rail failure from rapid growth of undetected internal defects. The Safety Board believes that the FRA should require railroads to develop rail inspection and maintenance programs based on damage-tolerance principles, and approve those programs. Include in the requirement that railroads demonstrate how their programs will identify and remove internal defects before they reach critical size and result in catastrophic rail failures. Each program should take into account, at a minimum, accumulated tonnage, track geometry, rail surface conditions, rail head wear, rail steel specifications, track support, residual stresses in the rail, rail defect growth rates, and temperature differentials.

As this accident shows, accurately measuring the level of rail wear is important in order to determine the appropriate frequency for conducting internal rail inspections. When investigators measured the accident rail using a template of the type typically used by railroads to measure rail head wear, they found that the rail head vertical loss appeared to be about 1/8 inch less than was actually measured. Because of downward deformation of the worn rail head under loads, the rail head on both sides of the rail web extended below the profile of new or less worn rail. The rail wear template fits under the rail head, and the downward displacement could have caused the NS to underestimate the amount of wear. The Safety Board concludes that downward deformation of a severely worn rail head can affect the measurement of rail head wear using a rail wear template and may cause a railroad to underestimate the actual amount of wear. The Safety Board believes that the FRA should require that railroads use methods that accurately measure rail head wear to ensure that deformation of the head does not affect the accuracy of the measurements.

Placement of Hazardous Materials Cars in Trains for Crew Protection

Twenty-three placarded ethanol tank cars derailed, starting with the 23rd car behind the locomotive units. The 3 locomotives, the first 22 cars (3 empty buffer cars and 19 placarded tank cars), and the last 41 cars (all placarded tank cars) did not derail. Because the first derailed tank car was the 23rd car behind the locomotive units, the train crew was not endangered by the ethanol that was released from the derailed tank cars. Therefore, the placement of the ethanol tank cars in the accident train was not a factor with respect to crew protection in the accident. However, because the accident train was a unit train transporting hazardous materials, questions were raised on scene about the number of buffer cars needed to separate train crews from the hazardous materials on unit trains.

Regulations governing the placement of hazardous material cars in trains for crew protection are contained in 49 CFR 174.85. The regulations specify that, "when the length of the train permits," a hazardous materials car must be no closer than the sixth car from the locomotive. However, when the length of the train (meaning the number of available buffer cars in the train) does not allow a five-car buffer, trains may move with only a single buffer car. Buffer car regulations were initially developed to address the risks of transporting explosives, which needed to be isolated from ignition sources and from the train crew.

When the basic provisions of 49 CFR 174.85 were developed in the early 1900s, main-line freight trains consisted mostly of a mix of hazardous materials and non-hazardous materials freight cars. As is still the case today, main line trains traveled from one yard to the next (sometimes picking up or dropping off cars along the way), where they were broken down and reassembled into other trains, or where cars were interchanged with other carriers. While the intent of 49 CFR 174.85 was clearly to mandate a minimum five-car buffer on all main-line trains, the regulation made allowances for short trains moving small numbers of cars during switching operations at or between yards. This was the basis for the allowance of a one-car minimum buffer.

Although unit trains transporting nonhazardous commodities such as coal and grain have existed for many years, 49 CFR 174.85 does not address unit trains transporting tank cars or other freight cars containing a single hazardous materials commodity. The FRA, PHMSA, and the railroads have recognized that buffer cars should be required on unit trains transporting hazardous materials to comply with the intent of 49 CFR 174.85. Because a unit train does not permit the repositioning of cars in the train to provide the five-car buffer (because all the loaded cars contain hazardous materials), the FRA, PHMSA, and the railroads have interpreted the regulation to mean that a one-car buffer is applicable to unit trains transporting hazardous materials. This can result in the contradictory circumstance in which a train of mixed freight cars with a single hazardous materials car must have a five-car buffer and a unit train consisting of all hazardous materials cars may travel across the country with a one-car buffer.

The Safety Board recognizes that the five-car buffer standard was not based upon any rigorous engineering safety analysis, but since the 1920s it has become accepted by regulators and railroads as a proven and effective standard. Although the five-car buffer standard is considered to have been validated over many years, the one-car buffer standard for unit trains does not have as lengthy a historical record and may not be sufficiently validated by historical data.

The Safety Board therefore concludes that without sufficient validation of the one-car buffer standard, the current regulations for the separation of hazardous materials cars from locomotives and their interpretation by the FRA, PHMSA, and the railroads create different levels of safety for crew protection from hazardous materials on unit trains and general freight trains.

The FRA has indicated that the one-car minimum buffer is justified and has concerns regarding regulations that will increase the switching movement for cars of hazardous materials. But unit trains typically involve switching only at the origin and at the final destination. Consequently, adding a specified number of buffer cars to a train at the originating yard generally should not entail additional switching of the hazardous materials cars and therefore would not cause increased risks. Rather, the additional separation could provide greater protection to train crews in the event of an accident.

Unit trains that carry hazardous materials present a special risk because of the high concentration of hazardous materials. The Safety Board believes that PHMSA, with the assistance of the FRA, should evaluate the risks posed to train crews by unit trains transporting hazardous materials, determine the optimum separation requirements between occupied locomotives and hazardous materials cars, and revise 49 CFR 174.85 accordingly. The Safety Board believes that the FRA should assist PHMSA in its evaluation of the risks posed to train crews by unit trains transporting hazardous materials, determination of the optimum separation requirements between occupied locomotives and hazardous materials cars, and any resulting revision of 49 CFR 174.85.

CONCLUSIONS

Findings

1. The following were not factors in the accident: crewmembers' qualifications, fatigue, drugs or alcohol, and the crewmembers' operation of the train.

2. The mechanical condition of the train was not a factor in the derailment.

3. The emergency response and the command system were effective and appropriate.

4. The derailment occurred when the north rail of track 1 separated under the load of the accident train.

5. The failure of the north rail of track 1 was precipitated by a detail fracture (fatigue crack) that originated from shelling on the rail head, reached critical size, and caused a piece of rail to break out under the train.

6. Rail surface conditions prevented the effective transmission of the ultrasonic signals, and the defect (fatigue crack) that led to the derailment may not have been large enough at that time to be reliably detected by the inspection vehicle.

7. NS procedures that do not require a re-examination of rail where there is a signal loss during ultrasonic inspection means that those segments of rail can remain uninspected and in service indefinitely.

8. The Federal Railroad Administration's oversight of the Norfolk Southern Railway Company's and other railroads' internal rail inspection processes was inadequate.

9. The Norfolk Southern Railway Company did not conduct internal rail inspections frequently enough to reliably detect an internal defect before it could grow to critical size in the significantly worn rail.

10. The Federal Railroad Administration's required minimum intervals for internal rail inspections are inadequate because they do not take into account the effect of rail wear, which can allow undetected internal rail defects to grow to critical size between required inspections.

11. In the absence of a damage-tolerance-based program, rail can remain in use with excessive accumulated wear, which increases the risk of rail failure from rapid growth of undetected internal defects.

12. Downward deformation of a severely worn rail head can affect the measurement of rail head wear using a rail wear template and may cause a railroad to underestimate the actual amount of wear.

13. Without sufficient validation of the one-car buffer standard, the current regulations for the separation of hazardous materials cars from locomotives and their interpretation by the Federal Railroad Administration, the Pipeline and Hazardous Materials Safety Administration, and the railroads create different levels of safety for crew protection from hazardous materials on unit trains and general freight trains.

Probable Cause

The National Transportation Safety Board determines that the probable cause of the derailment of Norfolk Southern Railway Company train 68QB119 was the Norfolk Southern Railway Company's inadequate rail inspection and maintenance program that resulted in a rail fracture from an undetected internal defect. Contributing to the accident were the Federal Railroad Administration's inadequate oversight of the internal rail inspection process and its insufficient requirements for internal rail inspection.

RECOMMENDATIONS

As a result of its investigation of the October 20, 2006, derailment of Norfolk Southern train 68QB119 in New Brighton, Pennsylvania, the National Transportation Safety Board makes the following safety recommendations:

To the Federal Railroad Administration:

> Review all railroads' internal rail defect detection procedures and require changes to those procedures as necessary to eliminate exceptions to the requirement for an uninterrupted, continuous search for rail defects. (R-08-9)

> Require railroads to develop rail inspection and maintenance programs based on damage-tolerance principles, and approve those programs. Include in the requirement that railroads demonstrate how their programs will identify and remove internal defects before they reach critical size and result in catastrophic rail failures. Each program should take into account, at a minimum, accumulated tonnage, track geometry, rail surface conditions, rail head wear, rail steel specifications, track support, residual stresses in the rail, rail defect growth rates, and temperature differentials. (R-08-10)

> Require that railroads use methods that accurately measure rail head wear to ensure that deformation of the head does not affect the accuracy of the measurements. (R-08-11)

> Assist the Pipeline and Hazardous Materials Safety Administration in its evaluation of the risks posed to train crews by unit trains transporting hazardous materials, determination of the optimum separation requirements between occupied locomotives and hazardous materials cars, and any resulting revision of 49 *Code of Federal Regulations* 174.85. (R-08-12)

To the Pipeline and Hazardous Materials Safety Administration:

> With the assistance of the Federal Railroad Administration, evaluate the risks posed to train crews by unit trains transporting hazardous materials, determine the optimum separation requirements between occupied locomotives and hazardous materials cars, and revise 49 *Code of Federal Regulations* 174.85 accordingly. (R-08-13)

To the Norfolk Southern Railway Company:

Revise your ultrasonic rail inspection procedures to eliminate exceptions to the requirement for an uninterrupted, continuous search for rail defects. (R-08-14)

BY THE NATIONAL TRANSPORTATION SAFETY BOARD

Mark V. Rosenker
Chairman

Deborah A. P. Hersman
Member

Robert L. Sumwalt
Vice Chairman

Kathryn O'Leary Higgins
Member

Steven R. Chealander
Member

Adopted: May 13, 2008

APPENDIX A

Investigation

The National Response Center notified the National Transportation Safety Board of the New Brighton accident on October 21, 2006, at 12:24 a.m. The investigator-in-charge and other members of the Safety Board investigative team were launched from the headquarters office in Washington, D.C., and from a field office in Chicago, Illinois. Investigative groups were established to study track, structures and signals, operations, mechanical, survival factors, human performance, and hazardous materials issues. The Vice Chairman, Robert L. Sumwalt, accompanied the team to the accident site.

Parties to the investigation included the Norfolk Southern Railway Company, the Federal Railroad Administration, the Brotherhood of Locomotive Engineers and Trainmen, the United Transportation Union, the Beaver County Emergency Services Center, the Brotherhood of Maintenance of Way Employes Division, and POET Ethanol Products.

APPENDIX B

Emergency Response Timeline

DAY	TIME	EVENT
Friday October 20	10:49 p.m. to 10:53 p.m.	Fire departments dispatched—New Brighton, City of Beaver Falls, Fallston and Baden Boroughs, Pulaski, Daugherty, and Rochester Townships.
	11:00 p.m.	Evacuation began with local fire and police going door to door.
	11:05 p.m.	Beaver County hazardous materials team bus dispatched.
	11:17 p.m.	Beaver County ECS notified CSX of accident and requested stopping trains.
	11:27 p.m.	Water authorities downstream notified of accident (Beaver Falls and Midland Borough).
Saturday October 21	12:07 a.m.	Foam fire fighting fire equipment arrived from Pittsburgh International Airport.
	12:12 a.m.	Pennsylvania Department of Environmental Protection on scene.
	1:20 a.m.	Water spraying directed for cooling the second derailed (24th car in consist) that was near a house (25th car on fire).
	2:40 a.m.	NS moved head-end nonderailed cars and locomotive to Conway yard.
	4:20 a.m.	NS moved rear-end nonderailed cars to Beaver Falls.
	8:15 a.m.	NTSB Go team arrived on site.
	9:00 a.m.	Two teams of firefighters and NS hazmat responders entered derailment area to assess condition of tank cars.
	10:00 a.m.	Responders considered stimulating the burning by pumping air into the cars to increase the burn rate of the product.
	10:00 a.m.	CSX train traffic returned to service.
	11:45 a.m.	Two teams went into derailment area again to assess tank cars.
	1:00 p.m. to 3:00 p.m.	Emergency responders planned response tactics and off-loading of product. Decided not to stimulate the burning of product.
	5:35 p.m.	NS contactor began moving the first four derailed cars and transferring product.
	8:38 p.m.	Evacuation zone size reduced.
	10:20 p.m.	Responders decided to cool the still burning 29th car (SHPX 206699) and use an aqueous film forming foam.
Sunday October 22	2:02 a.m.	Fire burning from the 29th car (SHPX 206699) extinguished.
	2:00 a.m. to 10:49 a.m.	NS contractor removed 16 cars from track area to a site located in an adjacent city park between the track and river.
	10:49 a.m.	Beaver Falls residents on Bridge Street allowed to return to their residences.
	12:30 p.m.	NS number 2 main track repaired.
	4:10 p.m.	Two cars still on number 1 main track and two in river.
	6:39 p.m.	Northbound lanes of highway bridge for PA 18 and PA 65 opened to traffic.

DAY	TIME	EVENT
Sunday October 22	10:55 p.m.	Responders began to cool the still-burning 44th car (NATX 301037) and use an aqueous film forming foam.
	11:15 p.m.	Fire from 44th car (NATX 301037) extinguished.
Monday October 23	9:21 a.m.	Evacuation restriction lifted by incident commander.
	12:50 p.m.	Last derailed car removed.